3 1 442

Upon top edge noted (c-car)

W9-BST-655

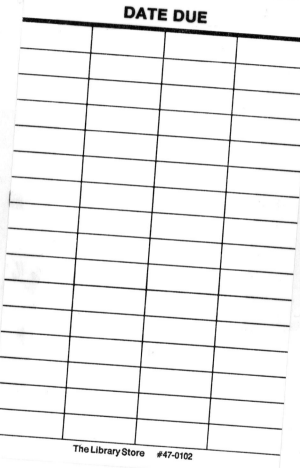

DATE DUE

The Library Store   #47-0102

THE
P I N T O
H O R S E

by Gail B. Stewart

Illustrated with photographs
by William Muñoz

Capstone Press
M I N N E A P O L I S

Printed in the United States of America.

Capstone Press • 2440 Fernbrook Lane • Minneapolis, MN 55447

Editorial Director   John Coughlan
Managing Editor   Tom Streissguth
Production Editor   Jim Stapleton
Book Designer   Timothy Halldin

Library of Congress Cataloging-in-Publication Data

Stewart, Gail, 1949-
  The pinto horse / Gail B. Stewart; illustrated with
  photographs by William Muñoz.
      p. cm.
  Includes bibliographical references and index.
  Summary: An introduction to the pinto horse, including its
role in the settlement of the West and its fame in movies and
rodeos.
  ISBN 1-56065-298-5
  1. Pinto horse--Juvenile literature. [1. Pinto horse. 2.
Horses.] I. Muñoz, William, ill. II. Title.
  SF293.P5S73   1996
  636.1'3--dc20   95-11253
                                              CIP
                                               AC

00 99 98 97 96   8 7 6 5 4 3 2 1

Table of Contents

Quick Facts about Pinto Horses

History

Pintos descend from the horses brought to North America by Spanish explorers in the 16th century. Pintos were favored by Native Americans, as well as European pioneers, for their beautiful color patterns.

Breeds

Since the pinto horse is a color type, there are pinto horses of many different breeds, including Arabians, **Thoroughbreds**, and **Quarter Horses.**

Colors

Black, brown, tan, grey, or **sorrel** (reddish-brown)

Description

The two basic pinto patterns are **tobiano** (a white horse with large spots of color) and **overo** (a dark horse with areas of white). A **piebald** pinto is black and white, while a **skewbald** is any other color combination.

Chapter 1

Standing Out in a Crowd

There are few horses as easy to spot as the pinto. Its coat of black and white, brown and white, or pale grey and white really stands out in a crowd.

Sandy is a police officer in New York. He rides a black-and-white pinto named Pepper. "All kinds of people come up to me—little kids, older people, even teenagers. I used to think it was my friendly face, but it's Pepper. Of all the horses in the park, he seems to get the most attention."

There is something about the pinto that attracts attention. Part of it is the horse's flashy coat and beautiful color patterns. Another reason is the horse's intelligence and spirit. But some people think that the pinto's history is the biggest reason for its appeal.

"People really consider the pinto an American horse," says one expert. "These horses are closely tied to the cowboys and the Native Americans of the Old West. Hollywood has reminded us of that in almost every cowboy-and-Indian movie ever made. But there's truth to it, and those close ties are fascinating to people. It's like seeing a little bit of living history in our modern age."

Many pintos have small areas of white color on their rumps, tails, and legs.

The color pattern of each pinto horse is different.

"There is something really magical about pintos," says one 12-year-old who owns a little pinto colt named Breeze. "I know that they were really special to Native Americans long ago. You can see why. Lots of horses are beautiful, but pintos are different somehow. They just have a look in their eyes."

Chapter 2

The First Pintos

Pintos get their name from the Spanish word *pintado*, meaning "painted." They are found in many countries around the world. They have a special place in the history of the United States, where they were important during the settlement of the West. It is important to understand, though, that the pinto is not native to America at all. In fact, no horses are.

In addition to a beautiful color pattern, many pintos have a friendly gaze.

Prehistoric Ancestors of the Pinto

Eohippus, the ancestor of the modern horse, lived nearly 60 million years ago in North America. This animal looked more like a dog than a horse. It stood between 10 and 20 inches (25 and 51 centimeters) high. Its arched back was similar to that of the modern greyhound.

Scientsts believe that Eohippus had a blotchy, spotted coat, like a pinto's. Such a coat could have served as **camouflage**. By allowing

This herd includes several pinto horses.

The spotted coat of ancient horses served as a natural disguise.

Eohippus to blend into its surroundings, it protected the animal from its enemies.

With the Explorers

The modern horse descends from horses brought to North America by Spanish explorers in the 16th century. These European horses thrived in their new home. The grass was long and green, and there were plenty of clear, cold streams. With such ideal conditions, the horse population quickly increased.

After the continent was settled, some horses helped ranchers to herd cattle. Others served in cavalry units in the U.S. Army. Thousands of wild horses ran free over the plains.

Pintos are at home in the western ranges, where many of their ancestors settled with the pioneers.

Signs from the Gods

Native Americans captured some of the horses. They learned how to train the horses and soon became expert riders. It was far easier for the Indians to hunt buffalo when they could race alongside the herds on horseback.

Of all the horses they rode, the Native Americans most prized the ones with spotted colors and patterns. They believed the unusual markings were signs from the gods that gave the horses magical powers.

The color patterns matched the color of the earth, of rocks, of a patch of snow, or of trees. This camouflage made the horses better for hunting and in battle. If a warrior or hunter was not lucky enough to have a pinto to ride, he usually painted his horse himself.

Says one historian, "Many Indians made markings on their horses' shoulders and rumps—as well as on their own faces—to gain the favor of the spirits of the hunt and battle. Marks like these were a sign of courage, both for the horse and for the rider."

Calicos, Paints, and Pintos

Over the centuries, thousands of explorers and settlers came to North America. Several new breeds of horses arrived with them. The English, for example, brought tall, long-legged horses called Thoroughbreds.

Over time, some Thoroughbreds bred with the smaller Spanish horses. Many of their offspring, called Quarter Horses, moved westwards with the pioneers. Some of these horses had the spots and color patterns of the pinto.

Pioneer families called their spotted horses **calicos**. Cowboys called them **painted horses,** or paints. In fact, one of the most common names for a spotted horse in the Old West was Paint.

A pair of pintos gathers to graze.

These new pintos were as popular with the
settlers and ranchers as the small Spanish
pintos had been with the Native Americans.

"The people of the West valued their calicos
and their paints just as the Indians did," says

Like most horses, pintos love to run.

one expert. "The reasons were different. Although the cowboys and pioneers didn't view the horses' markings as spiritual, they certainly admired the pinto's beauty."

Chapter 3
What is a Pinto?

Horses are usually classified by breeds. The members of a breed share common traits, such as height, weight, and body type. A Quarter Horse is a breed, and so are Thoroughbreds, Arabians, and Appaloosas.

A Color Type, Not a Breed

But a pinto is not a breed, it is a color type. A spotted horse of almost any breed can be a pinto. There are pinto Thoroughbreds, pinto Quarter Horses, and pinto Arabians. In fact, the only breeds that do not have pintos are large draft horses, mules, and Appaloosas, which have spotted coats of their own.

For this reason, it is impossible to give the average height or weight of pintos. A pinto may be a tall, sleek Thoroughbred, or a muscular Quarter Horse. A pinto may even measure less than 35 inches tall, if that pinto happens to be a little Shetland pony.

The colors of a pinto may be inky black, brown, tan, grey, or **sorrel**, a reddish-brown

Black and white is a common color combination for the pinto horse. This pattern is known as piebald.

A skewbald surveys his pasture.

color. The black-and-white pinto is known as a
piebald. A pinto of any other color is a
skewbald.

Registering Pintos

Although the pinto is not a breed, many pinto lovers want to keep a record of their horses. In the United States, two associations keep this information, which includes the markings, height, weight and parents of each pinto. Horse owners who are interested in breeding their pintos can check these lists. That way, they can find mates for their horses who will likely produce healthy offspring. They can also match their horses to mates that have similar color patterns.

The Pinto Horse Association of America (PHAA) was begun in 1956. The PHAA divides pintos into four catagories: saddle type, stock type, pleasure type, and hunter type.

The saddle-type category includes the Hackney, or the Tennessee Walking Horse. The stock-type horses are western pintos, such as Quarter Horses. Pintos registered as pleasure-type horses are Morgans or Arabians. Hunter-type pintos are bred from Thoroughbreds.

Another organization which registers pintos is the American Paint Horse Association. The

A pinto foal enjoys a cold drink. Many ranchers prefer to raise pintos for their fascinating color patterns.

APHA keeps breeding records, too. However, there is a difference between Paint horses and pintos. This sometimes confuses people.

To be registered as a Paint by the APHA, a pinto must be either a Quarter Horse or a Thoroughbred. Just as with the PHAA, horse owners who wish to breed their horses can use the APHA's lists of registered horses.

The Most Requested Trail Horses

Sheila Throndson lives in Alberta, Canada. She and her husband Roy own 22 horses, which they use to lead trail rides through the surrounding countryside. According to Sheila, her guests most often ask to ride one of their three pintos.

Trail riders like pintos, a type of horse with roots in the Old West.

"Roy and I have been leading trail rides for too many years to count," she says. "The pintos are the first to go. Everyone wants to ride one. It's interesting that people used to mention Little Joe's horse on the old television show Bonanza, or Tonto's horse on The Long Ranger. But since the movie Dances With Wolves, everyone wants to ride a pinto that looks like an Indian horse.

"One French couple that visited were really intent on riding what they called 'American horses.' We had already promised the pintos to other people. The young couple wouldn't ride anything else—they were willing to wait to do their riding until the next day, just so they could get the pintos!"

Classifying Pintos

Pintos are classified by their colors and patterns. A pinto pattern may be either tobiano or overo. Tobiano means that the horse is basically white, with large spots of color. These spots are usually on the head, hindquarters, chest, and tail. A tobiano's legs are white.

An overo horse is basically colored, with large white splashes on its coat. The face of the overo is either all white or mostly white. Its

A tobiano pinto has white legs and color on its hindquarters, chest, tail, and head.

back and legs are colored, as are its mane and tail. Horse experts say that the overo pinto is more common in South America, while the tobiano is found more often in North America.

Chapter 4
Pintos in Action

Because pintos are found in so many different breeds, it is easy to see why many people think that pintos are the most talented horses of all.

"You see pintos everywhere," says one rancher from Idaho. "They are good in racing, jumping, and other events. They are always the favorite in parades and shows. There's no event or competition that pintos can't do!"

A Rodeo Favorite

Fifteen-year-old Paul and his family have raised Quarter Horses for years. Paul's special favorite is a brown-and-white pinto named Sting. In the last three years, Sting and Paul have won 25 different rodeo events.

Sting is a Paint whose parents were both Quarter Horses. Like others of his breed, Sting has a sturdy, muscular build. He can maneuver quickly and change directions as fast as any steer. This is a skill that any rodeo rider values.

"I love competing in rodeo events of all kinds," explains Paul. "And I've ridden some of our other horses and have done pretty well. But riding Sting is special. He has a look about him that I trust. I've seen lots of other pintos that have that same look. Maybe it's part of being a pinto."

Pintos in the Show Ring

There are many activities besides rodeos for pintos. These are the more formal contests and competitions. How do pintos and painted horses fare in such activities? Just fine, according to pinto owners.

"I raise paints," says one man from New England. "They do well in competitions.

Most pintos are stocky and muscular.

I know some would disagree. But I think there's nothing more beautiful in a show ring than a painted horse going through his paces."

Some competitions are like beauty pageants. The judges look carefully at each horse's physical characteristics. Are its head and legs in proportion to its size? What is its coat like? The judges award points to the most beautiful horses.

"My horses always do well," says one horse breeder from Connecticut. "But I always find that my painted horses get special attention. They catch the eye, and they have beautiful features. I can't imagine anyone not liking these animals."

In **dressage**, riders guide their horses through certain difficult movements. Judges note how smoothly and gracefully the horse and rider work together.

A pinto owner explains: "In dressage, it is important for the horse to take a rider's signals, without anyone noticing. We use knee or hand pressure to remind the horse what we expect of him. "

Too Flashy for the Ring?

In the past, some horse breeders didn't like competing with pintos. They thought of pintos as too flashy. They didn't take these horses as seriously as a solid-color horse.

Skewbald pintos have colors other than black and white.

Says one expert, "There were plenty of judges and breeders alike who thought pintos had no place in a show ring, or a dressage competition, or even a polo match, for that matter. Pintos and paints were Indian ponies, or parade horses, they thought."

Another horse breeder agrees, but thinks that things have changed in the last few years. "I know shows and competitions used to be won by the solid-color horses," he says. "But I see a change. In some ways, I think it can be an advantage to ride a pinto. If you're a good rider, and have confidence in your ability, then isn't it better to have a horse that attracts attention? And I've never seen a pinto yet that didn't catch the eye!"

The Pinto Old and New

Throughout history, the pinto has been valued for the different color patterns of its coat. In long-ago days, when Indian hunters sped over the plains, the pinto provided camouflage.

Today, the pinto is valued because it stands out among all other horses. There's no mistaking the pinto, a horse that has made a mark throughout its history.

Glossary

calico—another name for a pinto, used by Western pioneers

camouflage—coloring that allows an animal to blend in with its surroundings and hide itself from enemies or from prey

dressage—a competition in which horses and riders are judged on the grace and smoothness of their movements

Eohippus—the prehistoric ancestor of the horse, known for its blotchy coat. Eohippus lived about 60 million years ago.

overo—a colored horse, with splashes of white. The overo is one of the two color types of pintos.

painted horse—a pinto Quarter Horse or Thoroughbred

piebald—a pinto that is black and white

Quarter Horses—offspring of Thoroughbreds bred with smaller Spanish horses

skewbald—a pinto that is any color other than black and white

sorrel—a red or brownish-orange color

Thoroughbreds—tall, long-legged horses brought to America by English colonists

tobiano—a white horse that has large spots of color. The tobiano is one of the two pinto color types.

To Learn More

Balch, Glen. *The Book of Horses.* New York: Four Winds, 1967.

Clutton-Brock, Juliet. *Horse* (Eyewitness Books) New York: Alfred A.Knopf, 1992.

Marrin, Albert. *Cowboys, Indians, and Gunfighters.* New York: Atheneum, 1993.

Self, Margaret Cabell. *The Complete Book of Horses and Ponies.* New York: McGraw-Hill, 1963.

Spaulding, Jackie. *The Family Horse: How to Choose, Care for, Train, and Work Your Horse.* Hartley and Marx, 1982.

Some Useful Addresses

American Horse Council
1700 K Street, N.W., Suite 300
Washington, DC 20006-3805

American Paint Horse Association
P.O. Box 961023
Fort Worth, TX 76161-0023

American Pinto Arabian Registry
P.O. Box 3
Lincoln, NM 88338

Canadian Horse Council
P.O. Box 156
Rexdale, ONT M9W 5L2

International Pinto Sport-Horse Registry
P.O. Box 7039
Sheridan, WY 82801

Pinto Horse Association of America
1900 Samuels Ave.
Fort Worth, TX 76102-1141

Magazines

The Pinto Horse
The Paint Horse
Horse & Rider
Canadian Horseman Magazine
Horsepower Magazine for Young Horse Lovers
Young Rider
The Western Horseman

Index